GROW IN WISDOM
A child's booklet of easy-to-read Christian doctrines

Susan Harding

D1808435

THE BANNER OF TRUTH TRUST

"And Jesus grew in wisdom and stature, and in favour with God and men." (Luke 2.52 N.I.V.)

NAMES AND NUMBERS

Have you ever thought how many there are of YOU? Why! Just ONE of course! How strange it would seem if there were TWO of the same person — or even 22!

And so, because there is only ONE of each person, each one has a NAME. The Bible tells us a lot about NAMES and NUMBERS.

 Did you know that GOD has given a name and a number to ALL the stars?

GOD has given a number to every hair on your head. GOD knows each one of His people by their NAME. GOD has numbered them all.

Number 1
Can you count yet?
The easiest number is
number one. There is only
one of you.
Everyone else is
different from
you.

Did you know that
there is only

ONE GOD?

There is no one else
who is GOD.
Everyone else is different
from GOD. Everyone else
is made by GOD. You
have one name. GOD has
many names which tell us
what He is like. GOD has
many names, but He is
ONE. The LORD our
GOD is one LORD.

2

Number 2
Have you ever seen a bird crying? A bird
does not cry. That is because it is not its
nature: it is an animal.

A girl or boy does cry. That is part of his nature: he is a human.

You are one person.
You have one nature.
You have a human
        nature.
Jesus is one person as
well. He was already
GOD. He has a divine
nature. But He became a
man. So JESUS has

TWO
NATURES.

He is GOD  in one person
and MAN   for ever.

Number 3
Have you ever kept a family secret? GOD has secrets which He tells to His family. Outsiders can't understand those secrets. GOD tells His people about Himself. He is ONE GOD.
But there are 3 persons who are 1 GOD.

Did you know that you were baptised into the name of

GOD | the Father
the Son
the Holy Spirit

1. The FATHER is GOD.
2. The SON, Jesus, is GOD.
3. The Holy SPIRIT is GOD.

Ask GOD to show you that secret.

Number 4
Can you add up
yet?
When one thing is added
to another it makes
something BIGGER.
When GOD is with His
people, they are made
stronger than anything else
Do you remember
Shadrach, Meshach and
Abednego? They were
just three men who would
not worship an idol. A
great king had them

thrown into a huge fire. How small and weak they seemed! But GOD came and joined them in the fire: 3 men + the Son of GOD = 4. With GOD, even the huge fire could not hurt them.

JESUS said where two or three of His people are, He is always there with them. Jesus' name EMMANUEL means GOD WITH US.

5

Do you know the story of David and Goliath? Have you ever wondered why GOD did not destroy that giant with lightning from heaven? What did GOD choose instead? Why, David of course — David the shepherd boy, and one of

his 5 stones.
GOD often chooses
little things to work out
His plans. MEN like
big things.
JESUS used a
boy's 5 rolls and
2 fishes to feed 5
thousand people.
GOD chooses
small things
  to show up His own
GREATNESS
  to stop us being proud.
GOD puts down the
mighty and lifts up the meek.

6 Number 6. Has anyone ever said you looked like your Dad? GOD has made us to look like our parents. Do you ever copy your Dad when he is busy working? GOD has made us so that we copy our fathers and mothers. Do you know that GOD is the perfect Father? He has done things for us to copy too. GOD was busy working for SIX days. He made everything in those 6 days. He commands us to work for six days in each week too.

We don't like to work much because we are sinners. We don't like copying GOD.

JESUS copied His Father perfectly. He did ALL the work He was given to do. NOW He works right-eousness in His people. Ask JESUS to work in you.

7 Have you ever done a jigsaw puzzle?  When was it perfect? It was only perfect when you had finished making it. There was nothing missing: it was finished: it was perfect. GOD made everything in six days. On the seventh day it was all finished. It was perfect. That was the work of creation.

In the Bible, seven is often a sign of something being finished or made whole again.
GOD always finishes what He does. He is perfect Himself.
Jesus on the cross said: "It is finished." He had finished the work His Father had given Him to do.
That is the work of salvation. It is PERFECT.

8 Number 8
I'm sure
you know
who built
the Ark ready for the
Flood. I'm sure you know
that the animals went into
that Ark, two by two.
But do you know how
many people went into
that Ark?
Noah and his wife
Shem and his wife
Japheth and his wife
Ham and his wife.

Just 8 altogether. GOD saved eight souls from His judgement of the Flood.

And do you know how many were destroyed in the Flood? We do not know that number. Nor do we know the number of people who will be saved from God's judgement at the end of the world. But we do know that JESUS is the SAVIOUR; and that we MUST repent, and believe in Him.

Number 9
Can you do
take-away
sums yet?
When Jesus made 10
lepers better, only one
came back to say "thank-
you."

10−1=9
9 lepers were ungrateful.

They did not thank Jesus for healing them.
People are still ungrateful to GOD. They do not thank Him for making the world. They even pretend He did not make it! That is sinful.
We should take every-thing from GOD, with thanksgiving. He has made US, and everything we have. We cannot pay Him back. But we can and should say THANK YOU.

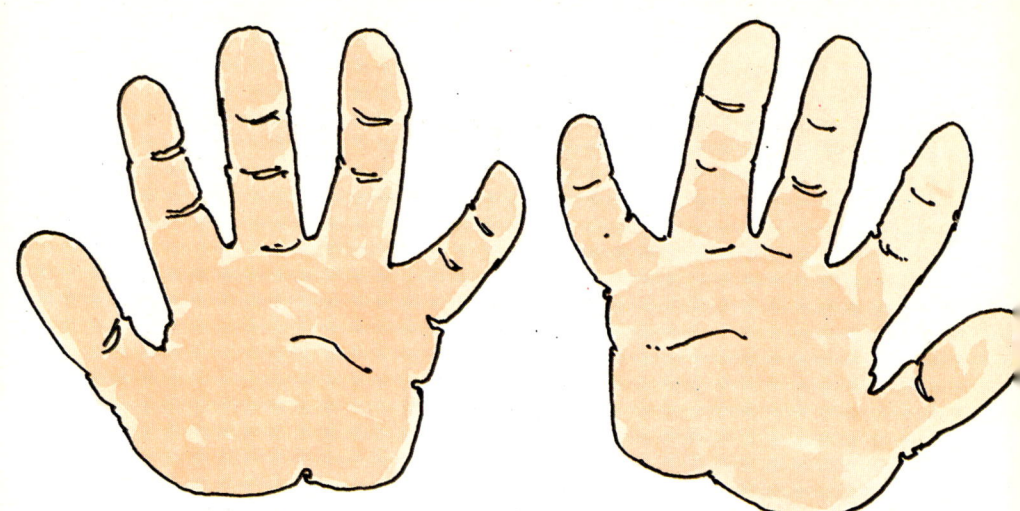

How many fingers have you got? GOD made us with ten fingers. GOD has given us ten commandments.

The commandments are a sort of mirror. They shew us what GOD is like: what He likes and hates. So, No lies: God is Truth. They shew us how unlike GOD we are.

They shew us how we do not like GOD: that is sin.

They shew us how we need a Saviour. JESUS gladly obeyed all the commandments, because He loved GOD perfectly.

A prayer to sing with the tune 'Crimond'.

Teach me thy way, and in
thy truth,
O Lord, then walk will I;
Unite my heart, that I thy
name
may fear continually.

Psalm 86:11